# How to be Heebie Jeebie Free

## by Karen and Christi Porter

Pawprintpress®
19005 sw 13th Avenue
Newberry, FL 32669©
352-514-8701
Printed in the United
States of Americ.

2

To James who helped us be heebie jeebie free!

There was a man named Robert Heinrich Herman Kich.  His fears at bedtime came in little fits.  Under the covers he would twitch.  He felt a presence under his bed unseen.  He imagined it to be scary and green.

4

He wanted these feelings to be set free. It bothered him so much that he could not let them be! He called them 'heebie jeebies', a feeling that was there that no one sees.

5

He found a way to see them the day he swam in
a pool so serene.  Nearby was something.......

gross and unseen.

6

A used bandaid floated right by. That feeling came back when it caught his eye!

7

The bandaid was on a man's leg and it really did stick. He felt it again that gross feeling of ewe icky ick. Then a heebie jeebie got behind him so very quick.

8

He swam away to enjoy the fine day.  Then his sister screamed "Hey, Hey, Hey!"

9

It was back. He felt it again, that gross heebie jeebie fear! A bug was in his sister's ear. They needed a trip to the doctor it was quite clear!

They got the
bug out and in a
jar. That heebie
jeebie feeling
followed them
home in the car.

11

That
bug in
the jar
would
take his
research
wide
and far.

12

He studied this feeling this bug made him feel. He had to know if it was real.

Was the bug the feeling? Did it cause the feeling? He put the bug under a glass case. He wanted to see if this feeling would be easy to erase.

He developed heebie jeebie glasses
to be used to help the masses.  He
gathered pixie dust and mixed it
with magic rust. At once he could
see this feeling he felt.  He had hope
now that a way to be heebie jeebie
free could be dealt.

He put on the glasses and tried to walk home. He saw his first heebie jeebie whan he stepped in some gum.

16

He saw it. There it was drooling
and green.

He wore his glasses home from the ballet, and saw another one that very day. His sister stepped in dog doo. It squished in her stockings all the way through. A heebie jeebie was there, and it smelled "pee you!"

He took a train to a city nearby. A man on the train was picking his feet and he didn't know why. Then he watched and he saw him eat a piece of skin. A heebie jeebie was right there above his shin.

19

Could others see this heebie jeebie? They looked like the felt the same way as he. He was sure they wanted to be heebie jeebie free!

Coming home from his trip his nose took a wiff of a man's soggy socks up on the air vent hung by a clip. It smelled so bad that he thought he'd sneeze. Now with his glasses he saw more heebie jeebies!

21

A man in seat C 3 could not hold his sneeze. Boogers came out with a Heebie Jeebie. The heebie jeebie was on the dogs nose, that only heebie jeebie glasses could help you to see.

22

That same poor couple returned home with him.
Just as he; they, too, wanted to be heebie jeebie
free.

23

So, he catalogued and watched them to learn how to unfeel them.

24

The stomach churning awareness these Heebie Jeebies brought, were spread from a thing of disgust.

Breathing faster, gulping, dizzy spells and sweaty palms, were symptoms he felt he had to understand, he should, and he must.

He saw they looked
how he felt.  They
could not swallow.
They always had
drool. Their odd
numbered legs
made him feel like
falling.

The eye in its
head was so
very odd.  It
had a strange
look that sank
into his bod.

They had odd spikes, fangs and horns with odd colors and smells.

They ate rotten food to make you feel unwell.

Dogs liked to sniff where they would hide.

29

They invaded his space when a strange bandaid stuck to his face .

30

When he first saw these heebie jeebies, it was too much to bear! He did not know how to get some fresh air!

After seeing all those things so gross and frightening, Dr. Kich had an idea that struck him like lightening!

There was an end to that feeling they gave you like your circuits were fried.  Something made them go "speep." and disappear when they died.

He took a bath and two dissolved.

He had a laugh and the rest went flaff. He could breath now, because they weren't even there.

36

He cleaned his room and went to pray, and even more went away.

So if you feel really creepy, and sense around you there is a heebie jeebie, you can spray them away with Heebie Jeebie Begone spray.

Karen White Porter is the Director of Loga Springs Academy. She teaches English Language Arts, and English for non-native English speakers. Her experience explaining words through art has led her to explore the many ways we use words to talk about our feelings with her daughter. More information about her Emotatude book series can be found on her author page at karenwporter.com.

Christi Porter is a lover of art, music, horses, and all animals. She is a member of 4h, Safety Patrol, and Girl Scouts.

Dear Parents,

This book is part of an Emotatude series of books that help children deal with their feelings. This book demonstrates how Dr. Kich identified his feelings and dealt with them. While Dr. Kich is a fictional character, he can help us think about how we feel and how we deal with our emotions. Below are some questions you may want to ask your child to help them identify and deal with their own feelings.

What do you do with your feelings?

How do you know what you are feeling?.

Why is it important to identify how you feel?

Does Dr. Kich identify his feelings? How? Can we do this?

Does Dr. Kich Identify how he feels? How?

Does he acknowledge his feelings?

How does he release his feelings? Can we do this?

Are there other ways to unfeel? Should we unfeel?

How does he identify the source of his feelings?

How does he comfort and reassure himself?

Sincerely,    Karen Porter

www.ingramcontent.com/pod-product-compliance
Lightning Source LLC
Chambersburg PA
CBHW041528280526
45792CB00004B/1412